To Sara
I understand that
we have things in
common! God is
directing your
and order your
and let him
steps!

A MIND OF EXCELLENCE

[signature]

Reverse Mort

Prepare, study, and achieve daily academic progress using spiritual principles.

A MIND OF EXCELLENCE

A Guide to a Journey of Excellence and Success

MARY A. HENDERSON, PHD.

A Mind of Excellence: A Guide to a Journey of Excellence and Success
by Mary A. Henderson, PhD.

Cover Design by Atinad Designs.

© Copyright 2014

SAINT PAUL PRESS, DALLAS, TEXAS

First Printing, 2014

The name SAINT PAUL PRESS and its logo are registered as a trademark in the U.S. patent office.

ISBN-10: 0-9915856-1-5
ISBN-13: 978-0-9915856-1-8

Printed in the U.S.A.

My people are destroyed for a lack of knowledge.

HOSEA 4:6

Freedom

freedom Po-on

cellphone

service Free

Propaganda

Can no more

Boris Lawyer

Contents

This book of the law shall not depart out of thy mouth; but thou shalt meditate therein day and night, that thou mayest observe to do according to all that is written therein: for then thou shalt make thy way prosperous, and then thou shalt have good success.

JOSHUA 1:8

.

A | Acknowledgements

Thank you, God, for putting me in a difficult situation so that I could do what You wanted me to do. Thank you to the greatest family in the world: my daughter, Emmettia. Thank you to Emmett, Ramona, Trevor, and Stan. Thank you to the greatest pastor in the world, Pastor Frank M. Reid III, and the greatest First Lady in the world, Lady Marlaa H. Reid.

I want this book to especially encourage my nephew, Leamon O. Harris, who has his hand on the door to his first academic degree only because God has blessed him. Thanks to Mrs. Cusick who went beyond the classroom to touch her student's life and support her student's mother, thus helping this dream become a reality. Last but not least, thanks to Lisa Mc Donald who sparked the flame that led to this book, and to Minister FranShon Reid for allowing God to use her to help me get the job done.

F | Foreword

And be not conformed to this world, but be ye transformed by the renewing of your mind, that you may prove what is the good and acceptable perfect will of God. (Romans 12:2)

It's time to empower yourself with a mind of excellence!

The conformed mind is a mind of mediocrity.

The transformed mind is a mind of magnificence.

God created human beings and gave us the gift of an excellent mind. Social and spiritual conformity has led us to compromise our passion for and pursuit of excellence. It's time to rediscover and unleash the power of A MIND OF EXCELLENCE!

Nelson Mandela, Steve Jobs, Bill Gates, Martin Luther King, Jr., Oprah Winfrey, Mark Zuckerberg , Jay-Z and Margaret

Wheatley have shown us how a mind of excellence can open doors of creativity, innovation and success. They have modeled for us the power of the mind to overcome obstacles and transform a mess into a miracle in the 21st Century.

In this important book, *A Mind of Excellence*, Dr. Mary Henderson provides us with a blueprint for mindful excellence. She has written a prescription for intentional excellence and success. It is the kind of book that is a must read and one you must share with others.

We need politicians, teachers, students, doctors, nurses, engineers, business leaders, workers, communities, faith-based institutions to embrace A MIND OF EXCELLENCE!

A Mind of Excellence is powerfully attractive because within these pages the reader can find a fountain of spiritual wisdom that echoes the voice of God in a godless culture. The scriptural references, coupled with the practical directions, allows the reader to walk through the word of God and activate A Mind of Excellence. Dr. Henderson is clear, A Mind of Excellence starts with God!

This instructional and inspirational work provides impartation for implementation. This book can be used as a training manual for those seeking transformation and a new way of thinking.

As we move closer to the end of the second decade of the

21st Century, we find that our world faces tremendous political, economic and social problems. These problems will be solved when people begin to think outside of the box of conformity and activate A MIND OF EXCELLENCE.

Thank you, Dr. Henderson, for writing a book that challenges our children and grandchildren to develop A MIND OF EXCELLENCE!

Thank you for giving all of us an opportunity to make a difference and change the world because we have been transformed by this awesome book *A MIND OF EXCELLENCE!*

Designed for Excellence,

Dr. Frank M. Reid III
Senior Pastor Bethel AME Church
Baltimore and Owings Mills, MD

Lady Marlaa M. Reid
Founder and Visionary
The Kingdom Women's Inspirational Network

Introduction

This idea began as a small project for my church which sought to provide back-to-school supplies for children in need. I was asked to provide tips that would help children get a better start on their school year. Well, as you can see, the thoughts blossomed as the Holy Spirit poured into my heart and onto the pages of this book. Thus, the creation of this manuscript came to fruition.

There is so much going on in the world that is negatively influencing our young people and their ability to think about themselves in positive ways. There is a decrease in the availability of resources for youth and young adults that can assist them, socially and emotionally, in their growth and personal development. There appears to be a significant lack of human contact and appropriate personal relations between young men and women, and the disconnect between the generations that came before them. There seems to be a disconnect between the church and the younger generation.

Because of the inability of one generation to connect with another, many young people struggle in their pursuit to find love, peace, and joy, and many appear to struggle with the true meaning of success. The older generations have not delivered the message that we need to deliver to save a dying world. These thoughts have led me to believe that there lies the mission; to teach all nations about a God who designed each of us not to accept mediocrity. There is the mission to teach all nations that God has divinely made each of us.

The mind was divinely designed to carry out the will of God. He is an excellent God and He gave you an excellent mind for you to live an excellent life. We must have a mindset that is centered on excellence in everything we do. We must teach our children and even ourselves to stop living less than our best and tap into the God-designed mind of excellence so we can live out the plan for our lives which is to live in excellence.

This book is for those who may need someone or something to assist them in creating a mind of excellence. This work is for those who need somewhere to turn to for answers. This work is for those who are discouraged, who have gotten discouraged at some point in your life, and especially for those who have given up. This is a guide to simply remind you that you have "A Mind of Excellence"! Anything you put the mind to do you can do, and if you decide it will be done with excellence you can make it excellent, first through a relationship with God and then through living out the principles and practices of God. This work is designed to help you find that relationship with God and pursue a successful life because one does not happen without the other.

Should you find that the enemy in your life is trying to steal your success, open the pages of this book and begin to fight for what God has promised you with "A Mind of Excellence"!

1 | A Positive Mind Set (Not Optional)

Believe wisdom and knowledge are things you need to have in your life (Proverbs 2). Believe I want these things (wisdom and knowledge) for myself.

Get your mind wrapped around thoughts such as: I would like to prosper; some material things are good and can lead to a better life; knowledge is POWER!

Think: "I can" and "if I want to," because all things are possible for those who believe.

Spiritual Principle: Proverbs 4:5: *"Get wisdom, get understanding; do not forget my words or turn away from them."* **The instructions you follow determine the success you attain.**

Place these principles in and around your environment to help you create a mind of Christ and to help you begin the journey that God has planned for you. The plan that God has for you will be easier to follow than the plan you have for yourself. Pray consistently and often; it will keep your mind positive and keep you on track to your God fulfilled destiny. You will be equipped to stand and succeed in the fight against the negative forces that come to try and block the way of your success.

John 10:10 states: "The thief comes to steal, kill, and to destroy, but I am come that they might have life and that they might have it more abundantly."

It is important that you understand that the enemy does not want you to think or walk in excellence. The enemy will tell you that you do not need knowledge to succeed. The enemy will tell you everyone does not need to go to school, and that education is not important. The enemy will set you up but you don't have to fall for the trap. The enemy does not like this message on these pages because the Word of God will help you to walk in authority towards your greatness, and the enemy knows that if you use your Christ-like mind, you will conquer and succeed in everything you do. Be aware, get ready for a fight with the enemy as you read, prepare and apply this mind of excellence!

Psalm 27:1 states, "The Lord is my light and my salvation; whom shall I fear? the Lord is the strength of my life; of whom shall I be afraid?"

The Word of God tells us that we are conquerors in Christ Jesus. He says we are victorious and we are made in the image of God. He is with us and we have the victory in Christ Jesus!

If you can accomplish creating a Christ-like mind which is nothing more than a positive mind set, thinking that you are above and not beneath, that you can do anything and all things through Christ, this will prepare you for any challenge that you will face anywhere and in anything you do.

Deuteronomy 23:13: "The Lord will make you the head and not the tail: you shall be above only: and not beneath."

Philippians 4:13: "I can do all things through Christ who strengthens me."

Your thinking will set the stage for everything else that follows in your life. Our attributions for success and failure are found to have a profound effect on the outcomes in our lives. Attributions can be internal, external stable, unstable, specific or global. You link your thoughts to your behavior or the causes of behavior. An example: you are a student who passed an exam; what is the cause or attribute for passing the exam, studying (internal) or the teacher (external)? Internal attributions are suggested to derive the best results, they are a powerful influence on the behavior that follows the thought i.e., what caused your success or your failure.

Attributions are what you say about yourself, that is what you internalize, what you believe about your ability, and how you see your future. Second Corinthians 10:5 says, "...bringing into captivity every thought to the obedience of Christ." Ask God to help you make His thoughts your thoughts.

It is important to monitor your thinking periodically. Take time, daily, weekly, monthly, or whenever you can, to reflect and evaluate your day, week, month, and year to see where you are, where you have been, and where you want to be. Even in the midst of daily situations you can be influenced by others' thoughts and actions. This distraction can disrupt your thinking and your behavior. When others are thinking and responding in a negative manner try and redirect yourself and your thinking back to the positive. Sometimes you may find that you may need to separate yourself from a situation in order to get your thoughts back on track. There are even times when you need to take time—an hour, a day, a month to step away from the situation (be still and see the salvation of God), and then revisit it (whatever it is) with a clearer mind. Allow yourself the time to process and to be alone with God in any situation that may cause confusion or discomfort in your mind and/or spirit.

Sometimes distractions, delays, or discomfort are divinely timed in your life. They may be divinely appointed to move you to where God wants you to be. Sometimes, if you keep trying to do something and it is not working out the way you think it should, step back, reevaluate, and think it over. Make sure you have asked God about it. It might not be God's will for your life!

2 To Have Success, Establish Routine and Get Yourself Organized

Matthew 6:33: "But seek ye first the kingdom of God, and his righteousness; and all these things shall be added unto you."

Colossians 3:23: "And whatever you do, do it heartily, as to the Lord, and not to men."

What does seeking the kingdom first have to do with your journey to success? It is the foundation of all that you do. Your daily schedule and routine should reflect that God is first in your life, and that you are engaged in seeking Him first before everything and in everything you do. The Word will not return void. You will see the benefits of putting God first when you begin to put Him first. It will be demonstrated in your life as you begin to evaluate His presence along the way in your journey towards success. We will discuss evaluating your journey in more detail later in this book.

Create a rhythm or a routine that would represent the way God would have you to order your day, week, or life. You will have difficulty in having productive days, as well as peaceful days, if you do not find your divine rhythm. Your divine rhythm is the way your day-to-day life flows in alignment with God's purpose for your life. You must pay attention to the things you are doing daily and write down the tasks you perform in your daily routine. As you begin this process of figuring out your rhythm, you may need to journal in the beginning. Take notes on what you are doing (your behaviors and activities) each day from the time you wake up to the time you go to bed. Keep note of the tasks and behaviors that you demonstrate in the day that contribute to a successful Spirit flow, and those tasks and behaviors that bring stress, negativity, chaos, and confusion.

As you spend time keeping track of your daily routine, practice removing those things that are counterproductive and those things that move you away from the Spirit flow in your day, that includes those thoughts that are counterproductive and negative. There may be thoughts and actions that require you to spend additional time working through in order to change them or to remove them from your daily life. Find time to work on those issues through self help or through the help of others, even if you need to call on a professional who can help you eliminate the negative cognitive patterns that you encounter on your way to success. It is difficult to put into words what flowing in the Spirit looks like because you have to receive the Spirit and spend time in the Spirit in order to know what is looks and feels like. Trust me on this one, no one will have to tell you when you are flowing in the Holy Spirit, you will know for yourself, you will know in your heart, when the Holy Spirit is present. There will be peace in what you are doing; you will complete tasks with accuracy and efficiency. You will be able to perform even when negative spirits are around you; you will be able to recognize when to speak and when not to speak; you will recognize when to get involved or when to walk away; who to keep in your life or when it is time for them to leave. You will want to note these times and use these notes to create your daily rhythm or routine that will lead to success.

I have discovered through my life's journey, the way you begin your day usually determines how your day will flow. The way you begin your day usually determines how productive your day will be. It determines how well you will be able to cope with whatever comes your way. The way you begin your day can give you the encouragement and confidence you need for the challenges of the day. Sometimes, if you are unable to start your day in the right way, that is, in the flow of the Spirit, you stop at that point of realization and start all over. The middle of the day is a good point to stop and reassess how the routine or rhythm of the day is going. It is a good time to refuel and separate from the world to seek the inner peace you need and to realign yourself.

Psalm 46:10: "Be still and know that I am God."

- Try to create a time schedule to do the same activities daily (i.e., eat, play, study, sleep, be awake).

- Make and use a monthly calendar (post it on the bedroom or bathroom wall, place daily, weekly, and monthly reminders on it).

- Ask others to help you stick to your routine and to support you in your schedule.

- Try and do most of your preparation the night before (shower, bathe, clothes, shoes, etc.).

- Revisit your schedule and make adjustments as needed.

- When you get off the routine, get back on it as soon as you can.

- Allow for play time and fun just as you allow for study and work.

- Allow enough sleep, family time, and restoration (most children and youth under eighteen tend to need more sleep).

- Use boxes or plastic tubs to organize (school

uniforms, shoes, socks, shirts, school books, etc.)

Ecclesiastes 3:1-3: "To everything there is a season, and a time to every purpose under the heaven: A time to be born, and a time to die; a time to plant, and a time to pluck up that which is planted; A time to kill, and a time to heal; a time to break down, and a time to build up."

Learn to use your time wisely. Time is too precious to waste and you cannot get back lost time. It is important that you become sensitive to time, routine, and organization. These factors work interdependently. The better organized you are, the more time you save. Routine helps to complete tasks using a less amount of time, thus saving time in the end. Understanding your time clock mentally and physically enhances performance and the successful completion of tasks in a timely fashion.

Learn your biological rhythm (body and brain) in reference to how they function at specific times during the 24 hour cycle of a day. What time of the day do you function at peak performance? Is it daytime or nighttime? What time of the day does your performance level lessen? When you figure out the time your performance level declines or begins to decrease this is the time that you do not need to perform tasks that require attention, processing, and other executive functions.

Routine: What part of the day do you need to create a routine? On waking up and/or when going to bed? Where should you be rigid, allowing no flexibility in your schedule? Do you allow yourself down time on a regular basis (too much or too little)? Is there rest included in the routine you made for yourself?

Scripture says everything has a season: a time to laugh, a time to cry; a time to live, a time to die.

Genesis 2:2 says, "And on the seventh day, God ended his work and he rested on the seventh day from his work." The seventh day was not given a name of the week, but it was declared a blessed day and God also sanctified that day of rest.

Cleanliness. You need time to clean your body and your mind. Clear your mind of the negative thoughts that have been processed in your mind throughout the day. Clear your mind of every thought that is in opposition to the will of God for your life. Any thoughts that stand in the way of your feeling good and having joy and peace, cleanse your mind of it. "Blessed is the man that walketh not in the counsel of the ungodly" (Psalm 1:1). Drive all fear out and all doubt that stops you from being successful in your journey.

Be careful of the little things that will sneak up on you during the day, that will change your spirit from peace, joy and contentment to a bad or negative spirit; beware of that person or thing that brings you bad news and always seems to turn your joy into sadness. Separate yourself from such people and situations. Find a space and an area in the environment where there is peace and stillness and stay there for a moment. This place, most times, may be a place where you are alone. It may be the bathroom of your school or workplace. It may be in your car. You may have to go into your office and shut the door. Wherever it is, find that place where you know you can be by yourself for a few minutes.

When you get off track or out of the routine, it is okay! You are human; you know that you are not perfect. Keep in mind that there will be times you will get off track. Do not feel guilty or punish yourself for getting off track. At times, you will not feel like doing what you are supposed to do when you are supposed to do it. This is not a time to beat up on yourself, but a time to forgive yourself. Forgiving yourself will allow that positive energy to flow and you will be able to get that positive energy that you need to get yourself back on course.

Forgive yourself when you fall out of the routine, but get back into the routine immediately. Keep the benefits in the forefront of your mind. Think about the positive outcome to returning to and sticking to your routine. Do tell yourself, "I needed the time, that is the reason it probably happened anyway." Now that you have gotten the time restored, tell yourself you can return to the routine. Announce the return to the routine to family, friends and those who are supporting you, and especially to those who are not supporting you! Let the people you feel will support you know your plan and how you are going to return to the point where you were in the process of achieving the goal. You don't have to elaborate, but evaluate who you are telling. This should be an easy conversation and if it is not, say what you need to say and move on. But whatever their response, go back to the routine plan.

Planning: Malachi 3:1: "I will send my messenger before me and he will prepare a way."

Even before Christ came, He had prophets to prepare the way for Him, thus planning for His ministry.

Whatever you do make sure you plan to do it for the Lord and not for man. If you plan to do things for man you will be disappointed and many times discouraged. However, if you start your journey with the mind set that you are working for the Lord when hard times come it will be easier to stay on the journey. Keeping in mind the benefits and what this is all about will not only keep you on the journey, it will help you sustain joy and gladness while working towards success.

Principle: Colossians 3:23: "and whatever you do, do it heartily, as to the Lord, and not to men."

Begin somewhere, anywhere. Just begin! You can revise and edit or delete later. Map out a plan for your goals. Gather people to support your journey. Gather any additional materials (books, articles, etc.) that will help you create a plan. Think through the plan and about the people you want involved in your plan as you start out with materials, an outline, calendar, or a list of the things and people you need to support you in this process. After you get this down on paper, revisit what you have written and revamp and revise. Tailor the plan to your needs, to your style, at your pace, and plan small steps, inch by inch, to accomplish each day. Revisit the plan daily and write out if you have accomplished each step by using terms like: yes, done, I did it, etc., reaffirming and confirming your efforts and building and maintaining your motivation. Use terms that are positive and encouraging to you.

Plan for prayer at the start and as you feel the need to pray, just pray. You cannot do this without prayer. Place prayer in the plan and use other resources to connect your spirit with the Holy Spirit so you can hear and see and feel what the Spirit has to say to you. The Holy Spirit will guide you and give you the plan and the Holy Spirit will carry you throughout the plan. Ephesians 6:18 states: "Praying always with all prayer and supplication in the Spirit, and watching thereunto with all perseverance and supplication for all saints." 1 Thessalonians 5:17 tells us to "Pray without ceasing."

You may also use a partner or a coach to whom you present yourself accountable. They can check in on you as the plan is developed and as you carry it out until you finish what was planned. Feedback from another supportive individual can serve as positive reinforcement.

Psalm 37:1: "Fret not of evil doers."

In the New Testament we are warned to "beware of wolves in sheep's clothes." Those are people who pretend to be there to support you but may distract you from your plan. Sometimes people see God's glory and favor on your life and they can't handle you being blessed unless they get part of the blessing. Some people cannot and will not cheer for you and your victories. They may be subconsciously or overtly jealous and envious. Pay attention and ask God for discernment. These people may truly appear to be trying to help you on your journey, but when you are with them, you are not on track. You detour engaging in something you did not plan to engage in or waste time you not do have to waste. Do not spend a lot of time in the company of these individuals. You do not have time to waste. There are people who will not go and cannot go where you are headed, even though you would like to see them go along with you. These may be people who are very close to you and your heart breaks to think that they cannot go on the journey with you. You feel empty and lost without them, but you must remember God's plan for them is just as it is for you -- a perfect plan. There is a future and a hope that God has for them.

Jeremiah 29:11 says, "For I know the thoughts that I think toward you, saith the Lord, thoughts of peace, and not of evil, to give you an expected end."

Keep in mind that everything will be just fine as long as you let God do what He does; you cannot do it for Him. God is in charge and He is going to take care of the person you are worried about. You are not in charge. Neither the burden nor the battle is yours; it belongs to the Lord. It is not your fight, it is not your battle, and the battle belongs to the Lord. Let God do His will in their lives and the sooner you let go of them, the sooner you will see things change for the better. Stay focused on what God is doing with you!

3 | Create a Positive Environment for Study

Second Timothy 2:15: "Study to show thyself approved unto God, a workman that needed not to be ashamed, rightly dividing the word of truth."

- set a place and space to study

- set a time to review and study

- avoid interruptions; share with a few others about your study time, space and place

- place materials and supplies you need in the study space for the school year

- keep your study space free from cell phones, ipods, and other distractions

- study with siblings, peers, others, or alone

- use resources to help you in achieving academic success (local library, computer, school staff, etc.)

Creating a positive environment is an important ingredient for success that we sometimes miss. We are bombarded with all kinds of distractions which divert us from focusing on or reaching our goal. There are many covert distractions that we do not recognize in our environment that take a daily toll on our mental energy. We are distracted by the business of life. We are detoured by material and misplaced values. We have no idea what is really important in life. We have our focus on things we think we need. There are things we think we must have but we come to a point in our lives where we realize, all that we thought we needed, wish we had and focused on obtaining, means absolutely nothing at all. This is a revelation that is revealed when we find the true meaning of life and its purpose.

Do not be ashamed to tell others that you have a set time in your daily or weekly schedule to study. Ask others to respect that time and to encourage you to keep the schedule you have planned to study. You may sometimes be bothered by what people will say and what people think about you if you tell them you are taking the time to study and work on yourself. It does not matter what others say; what matters is what you say to yourself. It is more important to be mindful of what you think about yourself because what you think about yourself will be the ultimate determining factor in the behavior that follows.

You will find that no matter what you say to some people, they will continue to distract and deter you from what it is you should be doing. Therefore, expect to find distracting people in any group or situation and prepare yourself to deal with them prior to having direct contact. You can meet a coach or peer partner to discuss confidentially the person or issue that is the distraction. You can meet a coach or peer partner to discuss these issues face to face or by phone. Discuss ways to handle the issue like using the coach as a support when you are in an actual situation. For example, have the coach or peer partner make a call to you when you are in the actual situation and use the coach or peer partner as a reason to leave the situation if a person is trying to distract you or deter you from what you need to be doing.

If you are studying at home, try and choose the same place to study daily. By setting up the same place, you will be conditioned to see this place that you have set up as your place of study, and it will trigger the study behavior. Even if you are not near this place you set aside to study, just seeing or being near that place will elicit a study response from you. It will serve as a reminder as to why you selected that place and will help keep you focused on the task at hand.

Decide your study modalities. What kind of learner are you? Are you visual, auditory, or kinesthetic, or are you a combination of them all? Do you learn best when there is music playing, or are you a person who needs total silence? Test yourself and see which modalities help you to learn. Once you figure the modality that works best for you, gear your learning to that modality. Again, use a peer or a coach to assist you in learning the modalities, specifically those you find are best for you.

Keep a supply of the materials that you will need in the space you have chosen as your study space. You may have materials including: paper, pens, pencils, and highlighters in this area. All of your texts and reference books should be in that one space. This way you remember where materials are and you do not have to look for them when they are needed. This also cuts down and reduces unnecessary distractions once you have started to study.

If you have not already come to this realization, let me tell you, the phone is a distraction more so today than ever before. People now have cell phones, ipads, and many other devices to use 24 hours a day, 7 days a week. I am not sure why anyone would want to be accessible 24/7. I realize that we all are human and at some point you must shut off outside noise. There are some people who just do not have any phone etiquette and who do not exercise any discretion in using cell phones, or other social media such as text messages, Twitter or Instagram. There is a time for everything (Ecclesiastes 3:1). There is a time to live and there is a time to die; there is a time to shut it down, and to turn off the noise. You do not have to die, literally, but you must die to the distractions around you. You must die to the world's noise. Make a decision that there are times specifically during study time that you will not respond to the phone, text, tweet, etc. You will shut it down. If something happens that is a matter of life and death, there is nothing you can do to change what has already happened. If it is a business deal and you missed it, maybe God had a reason for your not receiving the deal. Maybe the business deal was not in God's plan for you! We should be praying about everything anyway!

Philippians 4:6 says, "be anxious for nothing but through prayer and supplication with thanksgiving let your request be known unto God."

Turn off the phone; put it on silence or shut it off during the time you have to study. All you tech savvy people, create a message to say this is not the time to reach me by phone and let people know when they can get back to you or you can get back to them. Do not interrupt your study time to return a call or text, wait until your study time is over. You are entitled to have some time to yourself.

You may want to try and find a study partner or group (these people may be hard to find). This is also optional. Pray and ask God if you are to study with someone, or if this is something that God wants you to do with just His guidance. Sometimes God does not want you to attribute the success to anyone but to Him.

If you are looking for a study partner and cannot find a study partner or group, study alone. If you can afford to pay for a coach, it is worth it until you learn study skills and organizational skills as well as time management on your own. There are models in your community, even on your campus, who may have the time or be willing to take you under their wing. I am not referring to the advisor appointed by the school, college, or university, although these individuals are very resourceful. The school advisors usually are limited in the amount of time they can spend with you, and they do not necessarily advise on the matter of study skills, time management, and organizational skills. You may look at various community outreach programs and churches to find someone to walk with you for a period of time until you have mastered the basics of studying, time management, and organization.

There is a multiplicity of sources of information, and we are continuously bombarded with information whether we want the information or not. We are living in a time that information is infinite and all we have to do is access it for ourselves. The old saying, if you don't know you better ask somebody, has been overridden with, if you don't know, Google it! There are so many search engines and computer programs that provide you with nothing but information from any field of study or any area of life. There is no reason for you to keep wondering about a subject or topic. You are now able to tap into information at a few clicks of the mouse. There are people working in the library who are trained to show you how to find any information you wish to find, any subject you want to explore. The only negative aspect that comes to mind regarding accessing knowledge is that an individual is too lazy to look for it. Even if you cannot afford a computer there is one on your phone. If you don't have a computer or a phone go some place where you can use a computer free of charge such as the local library, school computer labs, unemployment offices, etc. Need Wi-Fi? Stop by your local Starbucks, Dunkin Donuts, or other places that will allow you to sit down and work on the computer via their free Wi-Fi. Ask your neighbor who has Wi-Fi at home. If you are trying to study, I am sure a neighbor will support that kind of effort.

Psalm 1:1-2: "Blessed is the man that walketh not in the counsel of the ungodly, nor standeth in the way of sinners, nor sitteth in the seat of the scornful. But his delight is in the law of the Lord; and in his law doth he meditate day and night."

Environment: Your environment must be a place where you can receive the peace God gives to you. It is not the peace the world gives, but a different kind of peace—a peace where the Holy Spirit dwells. It is a peace where you can be still and know that God is God.

Consider the people who are in your immediate environment, specifically those who speak into your spirit on a daily basis. The people in your environment should speak life and not death; they should bless, not curse. People and places where you dwell are to facilitate in keeping you in a position to delight in the law of the Lord. You should not have to fake it with people. In other words you should not have to hide your belief in God. It is important to evaluate your environment for ungodliness, speak the truth about your faith, but be careful when walking with sinners and scornful people. Create for the sinner, the scornful, and yourself an environment that exemplifies God and demonstrates your walk with the Lord as you think about Him both day and night.

Here are questions you might use to evaluate your environment:

1. Does my home/apartment/room reflect my belief in God?

2. Do the things I possess in my home/apt/room represent a Godly person?

3. Do the places I go represent my walk with God?

4. Do I surround myself with Godly or ungodly people?

5. Does my work place/space/office reflect Godliness?

6. Is there a place in my home/apt/room that is set aside for meditation with God?

4 | Building Your Self-Esteem and Self-Concept

Psalm 139:14: "I am fearfully and wonderfully made..."

First, let's take a look at how we define self-esteem. Self-esteem is an evaluation of what you think of yourself. You define yourself in a positive or negative manner by how you feel about yourself. You define yourself in terms of personal value and self worth. It is you judging yourself.

Self-concept, on the other hand, is the image or mental picture we have of ourselves. These images or constructs of ourselves are developed in many ways from our many experiences. Self-concept is also developed over time and can change.

When you have been or are being challenged in your self-concept or self-esteem, think about what God has said about you. Remind yourself daily about what has been written in the Word of God about you. We must remind ourselves daily that God is the One who made us and "marvelous are his works." This is what the Word of God says. This Scripture should be something you meditate on day and night in preparation for your school year or any time you are about to confront a challenging situation (before tests, exams, competitions, try outs, elections and day to day tasks). If you don't remind yourself that God made you, and He made you "fearfully" and "wonderfully," the world will have you to think negative things about yourself. Don't forget, if you are fearfully and wonderfully made your skills are also made by God. Also, your skills are fearfully and wonderfully crafted to serve any and every purpose that is in alignment with the will of God for your life, even though we sometimes use those skills to do things that do not line up with God's will for our life. You cannot mess up what God has willed for your life; and you cannot do anything about how fearfully and wonderfully you are made.

It is vitally important to feed your spirit daily and throughout the day. Think about the times that you attended church or you heard a powerful, encouraging Word and as soon as you walk back out into the world something happens to try and erase every encouraging word you have heard. The enemy is standing right there in the midst to steal from you all day, every day, so you must pour into your spirit all day, every day words from the Manual from which you were designed. The Manual is the Word of God. The Word of God tells you to live by the Word of God and every word that proceedeth out of the mouth of God (Matthew 4:4). I am your confidence, "No weapon formed against you shall prosper," because "you are made in God's image" only "just a little lower than the angels."

You must constantly work on developing and maintaining a strong positive self-concept and positive self-esteem. It is like feeding a plant. It cannot grow if it is not given what it needs daily. You are the plant, and you need to be fed. You need to bear fruit that demonstrates the greatness inside of you. The world system will continuously suck the life right out of you if you don't take control and use the power invested in you to keep yourself encouraged. The enemy has no trouble coming into your life and confronting you with negative thoughts and feelings about yourself. The enemy comes to kill, to steal, and to destroy, but God says, "I come that you might have life and have it more abundantly." You sometimes have to fight for your self-esteem and self-concept, telling the enemy that "I am more than a conqueror and I am victorious." Tell the enemy and yourself you will not stop and he won't stop you. James 4:7 tells us to resist the devil and he will flee.

Press on and press on and keep on pressing on especially when the mind is under attack. Know that you are fighting principalities and wickedness in high places which Jesus has already defeated. The enemy wants to see if he can confuse your mind and the enemy will tell you to give up because you are tired or you can't take it. The enemy is a trickster and these thoughts are tricks of the enemy. Jesus said, "I died that you may have life and have it abundantly!" Jesus said when He rose from the grave, "I have all power" and "I give you power, love, and a sound mind." Don't be tricked. Get yourself praying, fasting, and calling on God and watch Him move in your life. You are a child of the King and your Father is rich; He owns the cattle on a thousand hills. You are the product of greatness! You are given power, love, and a sound mind, therefore, you are able to operate in greatness! Therefore, you are GREAT!

Additional behaviors and activities you need to practice include:

- Practice being yourself

- Do a thorough self-evaluation

- Check your thoughts about yourself

- Check your appearance

- Check your behaviors

- Check your attitude

- Check your perceptions (How do you see the glass? Half empty or half full?)

- Check who you select for friends

- Check activities you are involved in

- Check who and what models you see as important in your life (from TV, Music, Video, etc.)

It is very difficult sometimes to learn to be yourself, but be who God made you to be. This may take a while to learn, but you must start somewhere. Try to work on developing a philosophy that the world has to take you just as you are in Christ, and you are in control of who you are and will make the necessary changes when you decide to do so. If there is someone or something that cannot accept you for who you are, then you need to move on. You must realize that you are not perfect and no one else in this world is perfect. If you can start with this mind set, it will be easier for you to relax and be who you are. Be careful not to imitate and emulate everybody including parents, because those you look up to may contribute to your self-image and self-esteem. Be careful when choosing those who you only know from a surface view. People do not present their true selves in the initial stages of getting to know them. It is not until much later and in uncomfortable situations that you learn who people really are. Love who you are first and then move from there. If you do not love yourself, you cannot love anyone else.

Think good thoughts about yourself: you are fearfully and wonderfully made; you are made in the image of God!

Consider the following things as you assess your daily

thoughts and thinking habits:

- Do you think on things that are lovely?

- Do you think on things that are of good report?

- Do you think on things that are pure?

Ask yourself:

- What is on my mind?

- What are my conversations about?

- What are the people talking about who I surround myself with daily?

- What are my daily conversations?

- Who am I talking to?

- Who am I listening to?

- What am I listening to?

Additional questions you might routinely ask yourself:

- Do I have positive or negative thoughts about myself?

- Am I spending more time focused on myself and less time focused on others?

- Am I taking responsibility for myself, my actions, my attitude and my behavior?

- How is my attitude?

- Do I dress appropriately?

- Do I behave to fit in or to impress my peers?

- Am I aggressive, passive, or assertive?

- Do I have friends who allow me to be myself?

- What do I say to others?

- How do I treat others?

- What words do I use in my daily conversations?

- How do I treat myself and others?

- Do I spend time with myself, my family, or others who are special to me?

- What places do I go to?

- Who is important to me?

5 | The Hurt and Pain that Come with Success

Not everyone is going to celebrate your success. Not everyone is going to be happy for you. Sometimes, you will find yourself standing alone with little or no support after a successful moment. You will find that others will be jealous and envious of your success. You may even find that people will set you up to try and block your success. This should not come to you as a surprise, although to some of us, it comes as a shock! No matter how much you hear the Word of God preached, you will find that there are those who are not listening as you have been listening. Others are coming to hear the preached Word, but are living by their own word.

The enemy will come on every side when you are successful and the hand of God is on your life. The enemy will come to kill you! He will come to destroy you! The enemy is not playing with you, so I suggest that you get serious with the enemy.

The enemy comes in various forms and fashions. He or she comes with a smile and a handshake. The enemy comes with pen and pencil to write down and take notes of your stumbles, fumbles, and fears. He or she will come at the most inconvenient time. When you are tired, weak, and worn, the enemy will come to visit you. He will come to work on your mind; he will cause you to become confused and have you worried about things that you should not be worried about. He will step into your finances and try to turn that into a negative situation. He will come into your family and work through them. He will plan to destroy you in every area of your life.

The most important area to protect is your MIND. Once the enemy infiltrates your mind he can control everything else. If you find that your mental state is weakened, immediately attend to it and reach out to someone whom you trust to help you. Seek help from a trusted friend, coach, mentor, parent, or professional to get assistance in assessing the situation and creating a plan to address your mental state. Follow through with the plan and have that person who assisted you to keep the lines of communication open with you until your mental state has improved. Even after it has improved, you still need to stay in contact with the person assisting you.

When you find that you have been hurt by someone or by some circumstance, what do you do?

Allow yourself to be healed from hurt, stress, pain, sorrow, loss, and grief. The Lord God says He is your healer: "I am the Lord God; I am your healer."

When hurt, pain, anger, and offenses come, how do I manage these things and still keep my joy? How do I keep my strength when I feel like the world is beating up on me?

If you are going to have a pity party, make sure you make plans for it. This might sound out of the ordinary, but we are not of the world. We are in the world, but we do not operate as those in the world. If you are going to cry, and sometimes you cannot help but to cry, do not be ashamed—go on and cry, however plan to cry and plan how long you are going to cry. Feel free to do so as long as you have a plan and an agenda to work towards—a plan you can think about while you are crying and work on after you have finished crying. After you have finished crying, get started on the plan. Press hard to get started on the plan. Getting started may be a challenge, but you can do it! Take small steps. Press towards the mark, the mark of the calling in Christ Jesus!

Plan not to stay down for too long and decide how long you are going to participate in the pity party. Stick to your time limit. Don't go into over time because it is the trick of the enemy. Brush yourself off. Clean yourself up. No matter how you feel, get up and move on to what it is you need to do to be in the will of God. God is there with you and will never leave you even when you decide to have your pity party. He will be at the party, but He will give you the choice when to leave. He will stay there as long as you are there, but He will let you decide when to leave.

Ask for clarity and strength to leave the pity party and for God to teach you how to walk by faith. Ask God: how do I surrender to Your will and Your way? It is easier said than done! But if you have a relationship with God it is like talking to your best friend.

Handling the Tough Times

When the times get tough in your journey toward success, what do you do? When people in your life, including the people at the college or university, at home, friends and family, or the one you love, don't see through the same lens that you see through, when they do not know who you know (the God of the universe), and they are not trying to live the life you are trying to live, what do you do?

First, seek the Word of God, find out what it says about your situation. Fast and pray, but while you are doing all of that, press your way on. Put on the whole armor of God everyday before you get out there (Ephesians 6:10), then don't stop until you succeed. Remember God is in control, however He will let you co-pilot. As you co-pilot, choose to take an assertive position and this will keep you moving forward even if you are only moving inch by inch. It is important that you keep fighting and never give up! If you allow God to take control, you will not waste your time on insignificant things. God will show you when you have to step back or go back. He will let you know it is okay to step back, but don't stay there. Regroup and move ahead. If you are not to move in the same direction, maybe you are to use an alternate route, tune your hear to what God is saying. If you are not to work with that person, perhaps, you are destined to work with someone else. If you are not to work in that place, perhaps, you are to work some place else.

Try to assert yourself, to connect, and reconnect with those assigned to your life's journey. People are sometimes there for one reason, one season, or a lifetime, so establish relationships that are working and moving towards your goal. If the relationship is not moving in the direction of your goal, step back and re-evaluate that relationship. That relationship may not be the relationship you need for your purpose at this time.

Be careful while you are asserting yourself, connecting, and establishing relationships. Be careful to treat people as God says you should. Remember there may be angels in your midst, and you do not want to be so assertive that you mistreat those you connect with along the way. Yes, be confident and know who you are and whose you are. Everything you do should be done with love even when dealing with those who talk about you, despitefully use you, make plans against you, place blocks in your way, or set out to discourage you. There will be those who will make it hard for you. Walk in the power and authority given by God, but be careful to remain humble and obedient to what God says to you in His law regarding your enemies. You will sometimes be tested and tried. An angel may be sent and you need to stay tuned to God to be able to recognize that the angel is there for you! Do not give power or too much attention to the enemy. The enemy is usually just a distraction to remove you from your divine purpose and especially when you are on the right track.

Aim to find strength from every situation. Count it all JOY.

Ephesians 6-11 says, "Put on the whole armor of God." Put it on so that you can stand against the devils that come against you. The enemy is the powers and dark forces in the world and the spiritual forces of evil that come up against us.

Am I aggressive, passive or assertive?

It is interesting to find that the word, **aggressive,** is defined in several ways including the definition of "likely to attack or to do harm," but it is also defined as synonymous to **assertive** which is defined as "characterized by or exhibiting determination, energy or initiative (dictionary.com). It is also interesting that the terms are applied differently to gender as I have experienced. When a female is described as aggressive this may take on a negative connotation. However, when a male is described as aggressive, it takes on a positive characteristic. Therefore, it is important to be careful and consider the situation before deciding whether you want to demonstrate aggressiveness or assertiveness. You may be perceived in a negative light and this is not how you want to be characterized. This is not to say that you are not to be aggressive or assertive, however, use these behaviors wisely. Many times, I have found that aggressiveness is not useful when it causes harm. You can be assertive when your purpose or goal is being blocked. You may exhibit these behaviors in a way that does not cause harm or leave negative perceptions of you. If you are walking with the peace of God you will know in your spirit what to do and when to do it. This does require maturity in your faith walk. This may be difficult to understand if you are not mature in your experiences with God.

Although walking in the authority of God may require some sensitivity, you cannot operate effectively in a spirit of fear because this is not of God. You are to walk and work with power, love, and a sound mind.

Passive is defined as "not reacting visibly to something that might be expected to produce manifestations of an emotion or feeling"; "letting others make decisions"; "obeying readily; tending to submit or obey without arguing or resisting" (dictionary.com).

Being passive, in some situations, is positive; and in other situations, it is negative. There is a prayer that says, "God grant me the wisdom to accept the things that I cannot change, the courage to change the things I can, and the wisdom to know the difference" (Reinhold Niebuhr, 1892–1971). Keeping this prayer in mind does help to guide you in knowing when to let go and let God make the next move. Sometimes we need to let God appoint someone else to make the decision. Specifically, when you are new to a situation or you have little or no experience in that situation, that is the time to be quiet and learn. Recognize when to speak and when to be quiet. Exercise self talk; pray and ask God when to speak and when to shut up!

There are times when it is more appropriate to delay your response until you have processed the situation. Don't be afraid to tell others, "I will get back with you," or "I cannot make a decision right now." Tell people "I cannot give my thoughts or opinions right now"; "I need to process this and get back with you on the matter." This will allow you the time to pray about it and to seek Godly counsel, if needed.

There are times when you are stressed and feeling overwhelmed, and this will manifest itself in physical signs such as, high blood pressure, weight loss, weight gain, excessive fatigue and irritability. During these times of stress, you may not be able to respond or communicate effectively. You may be responding passively when you should be responding with assertion. Instead of getting up you are sleeping late. Instead of having fun, you do not find any pleasure in anything. You must seek help and allow yourself to put everything and everyone on hold until you take care of yourself. Tell others, "I am taking care of my needs right now." The pain and hurt that comes with success can sometimes put us in the place where God can then teach us to care for ourselves.

6 | Mind Your Appearance

Be careful how you dress. This chapter may require the use of a mirror! Evaluate you and tell yourself the truth.

Do I dress appropriately?

Romans 12:1-2: "I beseech you therefore, brethren, by the mercies of God, that ye present your bodies a living sacrifice, holy, acceptable unto God, which is your reasonable service. And be not conformed to this world: but be ye transformed by the renewing of your mind, that ye may prove what is that good, and acceptable, and perfect, will of God."

1 Corinthians 3:16: "Know ye not that ye are the temple of God, and that the Spirit of God dwelleth in you?"

First Corinthians 6:19 states, "What? know ye not that your body is the temple of the Holy Ghost which is in you, which ye have of God, and ye are not your own?"

Do you appear to be advertising something? What does your appearance say to others?

Romans 12:1 says to, "present your bodies as a living sacrifice, holy and acceptable unto God which is your reasonable service."

Deuteronomy 22:5 states, "The woman shall not wear that which pertaineth unto a man, neither shall a man put on a woman's garment: for all that do so are abomination unto the Lord thy God."

Look at yourself before others look at you. Be honest with yourself when you look in the mirror. Listen to your spirit. If there is any discomfort, uneasiness, worries or doubt about what you are wearing, then most likely your spirit is speaking to you and maybe letting you know there should be a change. Too high, too low, too tight, too thin, too short, too much, too little—this is the language we begin to use when there is a problem with what we are wearing.

I don't want to spend a lot of time on this area because the world does enough of telling people what to wear, and this world has created some real monsters. The world has created a billion-dollar market in the area of fashion trends and it continues to destroy our minds with its emphasis on outward appearance and not on what is truly important, which is the inner person. The world advocates fake hair, fake nails, fake lashes, metro men, and the list goes on. Whatever is in your heart will show up on the outside. Decide on how you should dress using biblical principles. Spend time developing the inner being and the outer being will take care of itself. Protect your mind of excellence. Be careful whose name you put across your chest and think before you put someone's name on your gluteus maximus.

Use "A Mind of Excellence" and create a line of clothes that has your name on them!

7 | Face Your Strengths, Weaknesses, Problems, and Pain

Do not be afraid of your strengths or your weaknesses. You should know what they are. There are areas in your life that you must assess to determine what it is that you do well, and the things you don't do so well. In other words, it is up to you to determine your strengths and your weaknesses.

The smallest changes make the biggest difference. Weakness does not always mean that you are incapable in a particular area. It may mean that you need to practice or work on strengthening this area. Think of a rubber band. When you look at a rubber band its original shape may appear small and it may appear as though it is "unable to fit." However, when you pull on it and stretch it then the rubber band becomes able to do what you need it to do, but only after it is stretched. As you alter your perception of your weakness, you may notice your weaknesses only need to be stretched for them to become strong. Remember, we are constantly learning and growing. What may have been a weakness today, may not be a weakness tomorrow, because you have identified it and you have worked on it. You can allow yourself to grow and change, thus improving in every area of your life.

Identify your strengths and build on them. You are indefinable and unlimited. You are only definable or limited if you define or limit yourself! Seek to capitalize on your strengths. Use your strengths to create the wealth you need. Let your strengths shine and let God be glorified through your strengths. They are gifts from God and they are to be used to give Him glory. Be careful not to let ego interfere or get in the way with what God is doing with your strengths, which are your gifts from God.

One of the most prevalent problems in our success walk is choosing people to walk with us along the journey to success. Proverbs 2:12, 16, 20 instructs us as to who should be in our lives. This may be one problem that you need to address. Use these principles to help guide you in solving the problems or addressing weakness in this area. One of your weaknesses may be saying 'no' to other people, or not knowing when to say 'no' to other people, or even knowing who to invite into your life, or who to let go out of your life. There will be people to enter your life who will come just because they know your gifts are making room for you. There will be people who are going to tag along so they will profit from your strengths because they are afraid to use their own. Ask God to help you choose who to walk with in your journey towards success. You know that you have had enough of the user friends, fake friends, and pretend friends that came in your life because of your gifts (Psalm 1:1). Use God's principles as a guide to using wisdom in choosing people on this journey of success. There will be all kinds of people on this journey and it will make life a whole lot easier if you use God's instructions as your guide. It is much easier to just wander around and make decisions based on your emotions or your feelings, especially in this area of choosing friends, but you cannot trust your emotions or your feelings.

There is so much to be said about building successful relationships and building the relationships that contribute to success, however, when in doubt resort to the principles of God.

Exodus 31:3: "And I have filled him with the spirit of God, in wisdom, and in understanding, and in knowledge."

Rely on the Spirit, it will serve as your wisdom and will provide insight in making decisions. The Holy Spirit will guide you but the most difficult thing to do is to learn to identify and connect with the Spirit and listen to the Spirit when it is guiding you. This practice comes with having a long life and multiple life experiences with the Lord. There are no short cuts or quick remedies in learning to identify, connect, and use the Spirit.

You possess areas of strength and these areas of strength are gifts from God. When you are gifted and you know that you have the gift from God, do not forget to give thanks for the gift. Don't get so sure and confident that you forget where your gift came from.

Watch out for perceived weaknesses. Are they your perceptions, or are they another person's perceived areas that you have interjected and identified as areas of weakness in your life? Areas of perceived weakness can be used against you, you can unconsciously use them against yourself through your thoughts and self expression, i.e., I will never get it right, I am not good in math, etc. This evaluation of yourself may require a closer and more in-depth look at yourself. Things you identify as weakness may be related to persons or things you are missing in your life. Pray for clarity and insight into those areas. Declare war on the things that are contributing to perceived weakness and causing problems in your journey towards success. Fight the good fight of faith.

It is important to develop peace in knowing your strengths and weaknesses. It is important that you face those areas that you need to strengthen. Accepting your areas of weakness is a sign of growth and maturity. When there is no area in your life that needs improvement, you can consider this as a time when there is little growth, no growth, or no maturity. Identify and face the changes you need to make to make a better you. When others identify some area of perceived weakness, be able to let them know that you are aware of that area of weakness and that it is something you are working on. People will not be able to hurt your feelings in any area when you are willing to identify those areas of weakness and work on you!

It is important to find a peaceful place for you to go daily for restoration and rejuvenation and to restore your mind as well as to discover the things you need to improve. John 14:27 says, "I give you peace not as the world gives." Peace will keep you focused on what is important and keep you from feeling offended.

As you continue to work identifying and developing strengths and weaknesses, you will gain success. Know that there may be some pain; however, pain can be a positive force, catalyst, or motivator. Pain can put us into a place that is difficult to recover from or difficult to come out of, but pain can also birth greatness and produce plans and ideas. Pain can push us to fight harder than we have ever fought; it can show us the hidden or uncovered strength that we never knew we had in us. Pain can become a power source and propel us to success.

Finding Your Place of Success, Flourishing In It, and Growing Older

The place where you flourish may or may not be a very difficult place to find. You may flourish in many areas and this may serve as a distraction from determining the divine assignment.

It is my belief that you may begin your journey to success flourishing in one area and this success may continue for many years. You may believe that this is your divine assignment at this point in your life and then the appointment may change. You may spend half of your life in this divine assignment and then something happens to let you know that you have finished this assignment and there is another assignment for you.

Look over the journey, evaluate it, and as you grow, continue to identify and isolate your skills and gifts. There may be areas in which you can declare a specialization. Look over the journey and evaluate the past as you grow towards success. Continue to identify and isolate your skills and gifts focusing on your area of expertise. There may be an area that you can claim as your area of specialization or expertise. This is an area that you find you are most interested in at this time. It is an area you have spent years in study and practice. I am saying to take into consideration current time and current areas where you are more skilled and experienced because there may be multiple gifts and skills that you have been blessed to possess, thus you may be able to engage in many areas, but I believe you can engage in, as an expert, only one area at a time.

You must study, study, and study some more in the area in which you feel you are most gifted. Treat it as if it is a flower in a garden. The gift must be cared for in order for it to grow and develop and become the beautiful flower that it is divinely designed to be. It will not be determined by the speed in which you do things, but how long you can endure the journey to full development. Your gifts will make room for you. Nothing can stop what God has ordained! Nobody can take away a gift God has given. He will place you where you should be, and when you should be there. This is something you need to instill within because when you thrive in your gift, challenges will come and they may come to you in many ways and many forms, but you must stand strong in the power of God. If you know within your heart that there is something God wants you to do, a place God wants you to be, a place where your heart lies, then do what God wants you to do. Stay in the place He wants you to stay. Stand in your place of assignment knowing all things work together for your good according to the will of God and according to His divine purpose. If you love it and can do it 24 hours a day, 7 days a week, this is the place you want to stay. This is what you want to do. If you can do it without pay, without being asked, this is the thing you ought to do!

2 Corinthians 4:16-17 says, "For which cause we faint not; but though our outward man perish, yet the inward man is renewed day by day. For our light affliction, which is but for a moment, worketh for us a far more exceeding and eternal weight of glory."

Make sure what you are thriving in, is in agreement with God. Make certain that what you are doing, you are doing for God and not for selfish reasons. Be careful of the reasons you do things. God looks at why you are doing things and not necessarily at what you do. Be careful that you are not thriving in a temporary situation. Be sure you are not depending on and trying to please others looking for something in return. Do what you do for Christ and it will last! Do what you do for man and it will bring you pain and sorrow. You will eventually become disappointed and your success will not last. Sometimes, you will thrive for a short period in a particular area when man is your reason for the service. The success from what you have done for man will give you a false sense of success that will not last long. So reevaluate your purpose or your reason for doing what you do. Monitor to see if you are flourishing for the right reasons. Do not tell everybody of your service (Matthew 6:2). Do not serve for fame, notoriety, money, or other selfish reasons.

When we talk about specializing and becoming an expert using the gifts God has given you, we believe this is an area in which you have spent a significant amount of time learning and practicing. Your skill should be an area that you are very familiar with, so familiar, that it comes as second nature. You should feel like there is not much that you cannot address if asked about this particular area and you are up to date in the research and in the field nationally as well as globally. You must feel that you are able to function in the area of specialization no matter where you may be placed in terms of entity, location, or destination. You should feel secure and confident in your knowledge base and should have contributed significantly to the area of specialty in some way, through practicing, writing, teaching, research, and giving back to others.

You may reach a certain point of success where you are flourishing in your area of specialization but you may need to transition. You may need to recreate or move to a more mature level of work as you have accumulated years of dedication and are now ready to create some significant degree of independence. It is very challenging to move from dependence to independence. It is especially difficult, if you decide to be dependent in an area where you have achieved success for a long period of time. Remaining dependent or working for someone else in a particular area can create a false sense of security and moving from that area of success will require you to recreate the sense of security once you decide to transition into a status of independence or self employment.

If you are not flourishing, stand still and reevaluate. If you were flourishing, identify what has changed because there will always be change. One of the most important changes is growing older as you flourish. Be prepared to make significant changes and face multiple challenges as you grow older. Prepare for the physical and psychological change that comes with success because what arrives is physical and psychological maturity with the specialization and expertise that you have gained in your success over the years. Be careful in feeling that you have so much worth and that you are such an expert that you cannot allow yourself to make reasonable judgments and decisions about the realities of life such as maintaining success as you grow older. Be careful to consider yourself and those who are or will be affected when going through decisions of dependence (working for someone) and independence (self employment) while mapping out your success and career.

Plan to be independent and self-employed at some point in your journey. It appears that the best plan to maintain success is to start as early as you can creating independent success (self employment), however, you also have to make sure that you are gaining the knowledge and the skill to compete and maintain success that allows you to be self-sufficient, fruitful and multiply.

Flourishing does not always mean instant financial gain. Financial gain may be delayed although you may be flourishing in other areas of your life and flourishing in other areas without the financial gain may serve as the foundation for future financial gain and success. Millionaires are not made overnight, in a week, or a month. Money goes as fast as it comes, so don't try to hold onto too much and release too little. Giving and receiving is clearly discussed in the Word of God.

Malachi 3:10 says, "Bring ye all the tithes into the storehouse, that there may be meat in mine house, and prove me now herewith, saith the Lord of hosts, if I will not open you the windows of heaven, and pour you out a blessing, that there shall not be room enough to receive it."

Luke 6:38 says, "Give, and it shall be given unto you; good measure, pressed down, and shaken together, and running over, shall men give into your bosom. For with the same measure that ye mete withal it shall be measured to you again."

Don't let money be your measure for success. Scripture tells us, "The love of money is the root of all evil." Evaluate whether or not you are flourishing by answering this question: Where is the fruit that I bear? Count on multiple streams of income, independence instead of dependence, and be sure that you are bearing fruit; this will help you achieve and monitor success.

8 | There Are No Shortcuts to Success

There is a new wave in the younger generation, and this new wave suggests that there are shortcuts to achieving success. There are no shortcuts to achieving success. There may be ways to work smarter; however, work is just what it is—work, and it is not always easy. God's Word tells us that we must work if we want to eat, and it does not present us with a shortcut. It is specific when it uses the word "work." God's Word tells us "faith without works is dead," thus, just to think thoughts and ideas without the work behind them makes the thoughts and ideas of no use to you.

When you are given assignments, projects, or tasks in the academic environment or any environment, the assignments, projects, or tasks are given with the intent to help the individual gain knowledge, skill, and ability through the experience of completing the tasks. The purpose is defeated if the journey towards completing the tasks is cut short, or minimized. Because the purpose is not achieved by the intended individual, the individual has short changed himself. He has not learned what the task was designed to teach. You have got to go through the steps to complete the work to get the lesson intended. Many times we find that we have to repeat the task, we go through the same situation over and over becasue we did not get the lesson. We did not do the work. We have stood in the way of acquiring the wisdom and knowledge purposed for our lives. The individual will not obtain the knowledge, skill, or ability needed if the journey to complete the assignment is shortened. Ultimately, the person taking the short cut is the loser and suffers the loss.

To help keep yourself focused and on the path to success, think of the kind of spirit that is looking for an easy way to accomplish success and think of the kind of spirit that is looking for God's way to accomplish success and this will help you make the right choice when you are presented with a task in your journey towards success.

You cannot use deceit, dishonesty, and trickery to succeed. You will be a loser and will never achieve success if you try to use the short cut method to success. You must choose between the right and the wrong way of achieving success. There will be many temptations and many competitors, but do not let that intimidate you. Know that you are divinely made and you are made in the image of God and in the likeness of God, and if you are made in the image and likeness of God then you have everything you need to do what you need to do to become a success!

Learn how to put the enemy in his place without using lies, deceit, and dishonesty. Choose what is right, what is good, and what is pleasing in the sight of God. You will not only need to know how to compete and stay on top of the forces against you in the journey toward success, but you will need to know how to put the enemy in his place throughout your life to maintain your success. Know that you will be confronted more when you are on the mission to divine success.

9 | The People on Your Journey

Angels, Demons, Models, Mentors, Advisors, Counselors and Life Coaches

You will meet many kinds of people along your journey towards success: angels, demons, models, mentors, advisors, counselors, and life coaches. You may entertain angels. There will be demons, as well. Do not be afraid of the enemy and demonic spirits.

Second Timothy 1:7 says, "God did not give us a spirit of fear."

The people you meet along the way will be there for various reasons. Some may be assigned to propel you forward and to support God's plan for your success. These are the people you want to focus on and create relationships with. It is important that you take your time in getting to know the people who are presented to you along the journey.

It is amazing to look back and see how many people were allowed on the journey in my life, but what is more amazing is how few of them are there by divine intervention and who are willing to help you on your journey. You will find enough of them trying to block your success. You will find some people who will be on your journey to benefit from your success and these people are the takers, the parasites, they do not give and have nothing to give to assist you, but take from you financially, emotionally, physically and socially. Be very careful of parasitic people, they can actually suck life, health and strength out of you and you not be conscious of it until the negative effects show up in you emotionally or physically. If these people give to you, be careful that they are not giving with ulterior motives to use it later to say that they helped you. The people who give with ulterior motives are people who will take credit for your success. There are those who focus on your weaknesses and who will latch on to those weaknesses and prey on your weaknesses, sometimes for a life time, if you are not careful. You will find parasitic people to constantly drain you of your resources. Parasitic people will try and destroy your success after you have worked hard to attain it. They will hang on throughout the journey and will reappear even when you resist.

Be careful to focus on those people who are divinely assigned to support you; they will do it with ease and at no cost. There will be little difficulty in the relationships with the persons who are divinely assigned. Don't misinterpret what is being said here. There will be some problems but the problems will be opportunities for the relationship to grow. It will be a relationship in which you will not only find yourself growing, but you will be learning without stress or a depletion of who you are or detraction from your purpose. People, who have divine appointments, learn how to complement one another. They will learn how to disagree and agree as well as remain in a positive productive relationship even when they do not agree with one another. Some people will come into your journey and disappear quickly and some will come only to stay for a specified period and then there are those who are there for a lifetime. There will be people who serve as mentors, models, and coaches. Some will be resources and even suppliers of whatever you need to promote your success.

Today, you have more options in finding guidance; there are people who you can pay to provide life coaching. Be careful even when you decide you want to pay for their help. They also have a purpose that needs to be clear to you before you pay for the service they provide. Take your time and train yourself to wait and observe people's behavior in situations where they are being challenged. Observe the response in the situations that are challenging. When there is a problem that requires patience, endurance, honesty and humility. Observe their response in these situations. This is usually the time you will see the real person.

Observe people from afar and decide who they are prior to

joining you or before they come along the journey with you to success. Decide on those people based on their behaviors and not what they say! Decide whether the person has similar morals and values. Do they have similar or different experiences? What beliefs do they hold on personal issues? Do they compliment who you are? Be sure they are cultivating your life, sowing into your life, and helping you grow. Watch out for the users!

Remember the Scriptures that assist you in determining how to choose the people to travel along with you in your life's journey. Even when the people have titles, when they are professionals or have notoriety, they can be users and use you for their own purpose. Those who have been placed along the journey as a teacher, leader, preacher, pastor, administrator, guidance counselor, advisor, academic coach, friend, classmate, lover, and even family should be in agreement with your divine assignment and only those in agreement with your divine assignment should be allowed to come along on your journey towards success.

10 | A Conversation with the Academic Advisor or Life Coach

I want to take some time to talk about counselors, advisors, and life coaches. These professionals could make a significant difference in how difficult or how easy your life journey will be. Most advisors are there to serve people and they show you how to make the best of your journey in the arena in which you wish to succeed. Use your inner spirit, prayer, and experience to choose your personal advisor. Once you have selected your advisor, prepare a list of the subjects and topics you need to query, and develop questions you need to ask about your journey towards a successful career, degree, or period of growth and change. Ask for copies of books, articles, guides, etc., that will assist you on the journey. Create a folder just to enter data, information, and material gathered from the advisor.

Ask about any prerequisites that you should have under your belt before you begin the journey. There are always things you can do or experiences you can try to obtain prior to setting or meeting a goal. Taking on a new experience in an area that you are interested will allow you to become more focused and specific on what it is you truly want to accomplish. It will allow you to find out if this is something you truly want to do. It will even allow you the opportunity to change course. The question is, what can I do today, right now, to get prepared for success? The other question you might ask yourself is: What do I need to strengthen, or change in terms of my skills, gifts, behaviors and thoughts that would give me an edge as I move forward in my journey of success? We are all a work in progress and we must consistently believe that there is more work to be done on ourselves to meet the point of true success. We must persist in growth and change in order to meet with success. In today's world, change is constant, and therefore, you can never really catch up with the change that takes place; you can be vigilant in being open to learning and this will enable you to meet with success. Success requires infinite learning. When you feel you have mastered one area there is another area that opens up and begins where the last one ended.

A course of study or type of training you might be in need of should be specifically planned and followed according to the schedule designed or developed by the professional assisting you. A true professional can assist in mapping out courses and plans for instructional delivery, training or practice and it can be prepared by the professional prior to your arrival. They should be able to gather data or have the experience to know what order to follow for your individualized plan for success.

To those in academic pursuit, there is a sequence of course work for the person pursuing academics and it occurs in a specific order and the order is designed to meet a successful completion. Please follow it! Those on the academic pursuit are encouraged to take mini-mesters; they are more intense and require shorter periods of study with the maximum benefit in terms of time. Semester planning should be yearly planning. Don't do the last minute semester planning unless it is absolutely necessary! You should have yearly goals planned out a year ahead in the academic arena. You can find a specific course outlined for any area of concentration, major or degree. You can find them online or in a catalogue at most institutions of higher learning. This is usually in the form of an outline for a particular major or area of concentration. The plan shows you how to matriculate towards a degree and the amount of time it will take you to accomplish the goal. In addition, if you are in academic pursuit a yearly plan should be devised including the tentative graduation date. This does not have to be etched in stone, but set a conclusive plan, a plan for completion.

Even if your journey is different and you are not on academic pursuit or headed for other training or preparedness, apply the directions discussed to your journey and the result will still be the same—success!

11 | In Everyone's Life, There is a Test

Preparing for Tests or Exams

Plan! You must have a plan of action to maximize the probability of success. The plan must contain time and material involved in order to succeed. Reach out to resources or the source who is giving the exam and obtain all the information needed beforehand so you can properly prepare. Do not procrastinate or put off the planning preparation. If you put off the planning and preparation you will find yourself at the last minute trying to figure out how to properly prepare. This is where so many people find themselves at a point of urgency and procrastination, a point that requires more time and energy and a much more difficult place to be.

Get the exact date or the approximate date of the exam and the exact or almost exact material needed to study for the exam. This requires conversing with the source, the person giving the exam. Don't assume, but go straight to the source.

Many of us guess and assume what will be on an exam, and we usually are close but not close enough. The easiest way to solve this issue of what to study for an exam is to ask, pay attention during class time, and do your required reading throughout the semester.

In preparing and planning for the exam, start by counting the days from the time you are to start to study to the last day you have to study for the exam. Divide the material you will need to cover across the counted days. If it involves textbooks chapters, count the number of pages and divide by the number of days you have to study and this will give you the minimum you will have to cover each day in the time you have to study. Studying should begin from the first day of class. You can increase the likelihood of success by reading the assigned material ahead of time. This will give you a better understanding of the material which should support your learning and comprehension in any given assignment.

In other words, review the material you have to study just to determine a count of how much time (in days) it will take you to study the material in a given amount of days. Divide the total amount of material by the number of days you have to study. Use a calendar to plan how much material you will cover each day within the number of days you have to study up to the day of the exam.

Start your studies! Getting started is the hardest part, but once you get started it becomes easier to continue if you eliminate distractions. Stick to your study schedule. You will become conditioned to studying if you set yourself up with the reinforcers we discussed in chapter two.

Tell people, "I am studying. I will not be available until this time. Be disciplined, study same time, same day, and same place and according to your time schedule. Do not do less. Try to have a minimum time to study, and if you go over that time, that is better than going below the minimum. You set the schedule and you stick to it.

It is not recommended to do more than 1 1/2 or 2 hours per study session; studying longer hours is not beneficial due to our biological brain design. Many find it difficult to focus for more than 2 hours at a time. Determine what works for you. Implement breaks as needed.

Additional factors should be considered on an individualized basis and developed based on the individual's learning modalities. Identify your best learning modality. Are you visual, auditory, tactile, kinesthetic or a combination? Determine what your best modality for learning is and use it to study.

If you are a visual learner try techniques including highlighting the major points, underlining phrases and words, creating a vocabulary list and using flash cards. Auditory learners may benefit from CDs and tapes.

Apply what you are studying to daily life to make it more meaningful. When learning is coded in the deepest level of the memory it is referred to as the semantic level of memory. At this level, memory is stored permanently, and this is the best level of learning. Learning on the semantic level is known as elaborate rehearsal. Elaborate rehearsal is the rehearsal of old and new information, but the important process in elaborate rehearsal is making a connection or relationship between the old information and the new information to be stored permanently. This is a level that requires you to store the information and connect the new material as it relates to old material that allows you to be able to store the information for retrieval.

Use mnemonics and acronyms, as well as acrostics and other techniques to help you remember. Mnemonics are using things that you can remember easily through changing the information in a way that is fun and easy to recall. An acronym is formed by using the first letter of any piece of information that has to be learned and it helps to recall that information easily, such as the acronym "HBCUs" which stands for Historically Black Colleges and Universities. An acrostic is a phrase that you use for the same purpose, but you create a phrase to recall the information instead of using the first letters.

Create vocabulary lists that are directly related to the discipline you are studying. For example, lawyers have legal terminologies unlike the discipline of a physician. As you review the area of study, learn the important terminology that is significant to the discipline or subject. Specific subjects or disciplines have their own language or terminologies and sometimes it is just a matter of learning and understanding the terminologies, concepts, and or words used in that particular discipline. If there is a specific use of terminology, focus on the kinds of terms that are related to that area or discipline and surround yourself with others who can speak the language of the discipline proficiently. You will find that you will learn more from associating with those fluent in the language of that particular discipline. Have daily conversations and engage in conversation with someone who understands slightly more and who is willing to work with you on the terminologies and concepts in the discipline to advance you to their level.

I cannot express in words how important it is to create a time for prayer and meditation as well as obtain motivation from the Word of God and/or hear the Word of God daily in all that you do.

In Conclusion

What is success? I believe the divine purpose for your life is success. How do we achieve success? I believe seeking the kingdom first and working in an excellent way will always lead us to success. A positive mind set is not optional. It is required if you are to have success, establish routine get yourself organized, and create a plan. Create a positive environment for studying, building your self-esteem and self-concept. Tough times will come, and it is how you handle them when they come that counts. How do you look on the outside? Does it match the inside? Face your strengths, weaknesses, problems, and pain. The place where you thrive is usually your assignment; just know that change will come. Know your place of success; try and understand the people who should accompany you on your journey including the angels, demons, models, mentors, advisors, counselors, and life coaches. **A conversation with the best advisor is a conversation with the King. He will prepare you for anything—an upcoming test or a major exam.** Get prepared because there will always be a test in your life. However, if you work in an excellent way, this will always lead to success!

Journal Section

<u>Goals for the year:</u>

- Set goals for the new academic year.

- Be specific when you write your goals.

- When and how will you achieve these goals?

What do you need to do to achieve the goals?

- Review the goals quarterly.

- Adjust goals as needed.

- Follow up and measure if you have or have not achieved the goal.

- Ask why or why not?

12 | Journal

This portion of the book will allow the space you need to keep a daily journal for at least the first 180 days of a school year or even 365 days, a complete year of study and planning. You can journal throughout a specific project or idea that you are pursuing or working through. Use this through your school years or while you are in the pursuit of a secondary education. For those of you who are seeking private practice and are working for yourself or even ministering to others, you may want to journal and save the journal to assist you or to assist others in the journey towards success.

There are some additional activities here for you to consider that will increase your potential for success. You may want to carry this book with you in order to make use of the activities and to journal. Taking the time to use the notes you journal here will give you a chance to see your journey in retrospect. Use the journal as a tool for evaluation and reevaluation as you begin or continue your journey to success.

1. List your goals for the year (the next five years).

1. _____

2. _____

3. _____

4. _____

5. _____

2. How will you achieve these goals. (Write this out as you visualize it.)

1. _____

2. _____

3. _____

4. _____

5. _____

3. List the people who will help you this year and get contact information from them to keep as a resource.

1. _____

2. _____

3. _____

4. _____

5. _____

4. List your areas of strength.

1. _____

2. _____

3. _____

4. _____

5. _____

5. List your areas of weakness.

1. _____

2. _____

3. _____

4. _____

5. _____

6. List work you can complete in preparation to reach your goals.

1. _____

2. _____

3. _____

4. _____

5. _____

7. List websites that will be helpful in each subject area.

1. _____

2. _____

3. _____

4. _____

5. _____

8. List books that you will read about your culture or that are of interest to you.

1. _____

2. _____

3. _____

4. _____

5. _____

9. List workshops, seminars, and conferences that will teach you about your area of interest.

1. _____

2. _____

3. _____

4. _____

5. _____

10. List person(s) or place(s) where you will volunteer your time or talent this year.

1. _____

2. _____

3. _____

4. _____

5. _____

11. List people who you will consider asking to mentor you, where you might intern, or who you might use as a model to achieve your goals.

1. _____

2. _____

3. _____

4. _____

5. _____

12. List those who will feed you spiritually (give specific days and times).

1. _____

2. _____

3. _____

4. _____

5. _____

13. What days are set aside for study?

1. _____

2. _____

3. _____

4. _____

5. _____

14. What days and times are set aside for prayer?

1. _____

2. _____

3. _____

4. _____

5. _____

15. When can I fast?

1. _____

2. _____

3. _____

4. _____

5. _____

16. When will I break, rest, and/or take a vacation?

1. _____

2. _____

3. _____

4. _____

5. _____

Journal

Journal

Journal

Journal

Journal

Journal

Journal

Journal

Journal

Journal

Journal

Journal

Journal

Journal

Journal

Journal

Journal

Journal

Journal

Journal

Journal

Journal

Journal

Journal

Journal

Journal

Journal

Journal

Journal

Journal

Journal

Journal

Journal

Journal

Journal

Journal

Journal

Journal

"Home Advisor.com for people to hire to work at home"

Hughes is not for a challenge to a hard work